THE BOSTON MASSACRE

A one-act drama by
Ed Shockley

COPYRIGHT RULES TO REMEMBER

CAST OF CHARACTERS

The play is performed as a surreal event with a company of actors playing and replaying the same event from different perspectives. Masks or iconic costume items can be used in place of assigning specific roles to individual actors. Lines assigned to chorus can be divided among existing characters or used to expand the number in the show.

THE PAINTER
CRISPUS ATTUCKS
SAMUEL GRAY
JAMES CALDWELL
SAMUEL MAVERICK
PATRICK CARR
KID
CHRISTOPHER MONK
MIDWIFE
MRS. MAVERICK
EDWARD GARRICK
BARTHOLOMEW BROADERS
JOHN ADAMS
PROSECUTOR PAINE
MR. ASTON
MR. BRIDGHAM
REVEREND
MOTHER CARR
MOTHER CALDWELL
MIDWIFE
MR. BASS
MR. FOSDICK

JAMES BAILEY
SERVING WOMAN
SHERIFF
SEAMAN

BRITISH SOLDIERS

CAPTAIN THOMAS PRESTON
PRIVATE HUGH WHITE
CAPTAIN JOHN GOLDFINCH
CORPORAL WARREN WEEMS
LIEUTENANT JAMES BASSET
PRIVATE H. MONTGOMERY
PRIVATE MATTHEW KILLROY
PRIVATE WILLIAM WARREN
PRIVATE HAMMOND GREEN
PRIVATE JOHN MONROE
PRIVATE THOMAS GREENWOOD
PRIVATE WILLIAM MCCAULEY
PRIVATE JOHN HARTEGAN

OFFICIALS

MR HASTINGS, Acting Lieutenant Governor
JUDGE #1, Justice Benjamin Lynde
JUDGE #2, Justice John Cushing
JUDGE #3, Justice Peter Oliver
JUDGE, Justice Edmund Trowerbridge

The flexible ensemble also plays Townspeople, Colonists, Commanders, Soldiers, Delegates and Jurors. Lines may be assigned however best fits your production.

(The stage is dark. A PAINTER appears in a nowhere defined by light.)

PAINTER: Something within me loathes an empty canvas. The boundless possibility that is immediately diluted with the application of the first swath of...red.

(She brushes the air with her hand and defines the red back of a character.)

Suddenly the perfection that had been suspended just beyond the horsehair bristles of my brush is transformed into a...what? A soldier...a British soldier...standing guard...Where? ...In front of a quaint...brick...colonial...custom house.

(She paints and the building appears behind the soldier.)

And the soldier has an enemy...and the enemy is armed...

(CRISPUS ATTUCKS appears with a rifle.)

but this is not a battle of equals. He has no gun...He has a pathetic, knotty, block of wood...

(Attucks reluctantly surrenders the gun and takes a block of wood.)

And there are hordes of angry, frightened people on both sides but how, and why, and who and where?

(The entire scene appears and animates and the Painter sits and studies the tableau.)

COLONIST SAMUEL GRAY: It was loud.

COLONIST JAMES CALDWELL: The noise.

COLONIST SAMUEL MAVERICK: Musket fire.

LIEUTENANT BASSET: Screaming.

CRISPUS ATTUCKS: So much blood.

COLONIST PATRICK CARR: Running!

KID: I'm afraid.

COLONIST BARTHOLOMEW BROADERS: Snowballs.

COLONIST EDWARD GARRICK: Sticks.

PRIVATE WHITE: Cudgels.

CARR: Sod King George!

LT. BASSET: Vile insults!

COLONIST CHRISTOPHER MONK: Bloody bayonets.

MIDWIFE: Bloody hands!

MRS. MAVERICK: Bloody heathens!

SOLDIERS: Bloody!

PATRIOTS: Bloody!

ALL: Bloody madness!

(There is an explosion of guns, screams and chaos, then everyone freezes as the Painter reappears.)

PAINTER: No! This doesn't tell the story. Somehow I must pass beyond the bluster of the moment and capture its' meaning. Perhaps a single figure of great significance. One who is central to the tragedy. Someone like the officer responsible for the soldiers.

(She creates CAPTAIN PRESTON.)

A portrait perhaps of the humorless captain who must report the deaths of five civilians to some unseen superior who looms ominously just beyond the canvas frame awaiting explanation for the grim deeds of this day.

(A CHORUS OF FACELESS COMMANDERS move in and out of the shadows.)

CHORUS OF COMMANDERS: Captain Preston!

CAPTAIN PRESTON: Sirrah!

CHORUS OF COMMANDERS: Your report.

CAPTAIN PRESTON: I was duty officer at the State Custom House, Boston, on the fifth day March last, year of our Lord seventeen hundred and seventy. It had been an uneventful watch until a disquieting din brought me out from the barracks where I found one of my men menaced by an unruly mob of hooligans numbering two or more score. Invectives, threats, treacherous ice balls, all were hurled at my courageous charges whom, in obeisance to our standing orders regarding colonists, held their ground and withheld their fire. The situation was exceedingly volatile, as the mob taunted and even snatched at the weapons of my troops, wholly disregarding the deadly bayonets that could have dispatched the lot on my command. There was energetic jostling at the front of the fray, and someone discharged a firearm. No order had been given, and it is entirely impossible to ascertain which side inaugurated the escalation in hostilities. The attackers were repulsed at the cost of four lives and several wounded.

PAINTER: Visually this gives me nothing, just a captain standing at attention.

(Actors create the picture that she describes.)

I might add figures from his report as a backdrop to his pronouncements, perhaps seat him at a table writing the letter that must lugubriously cross the Atlantic to his superiors and King but I am better served to find some image that captures the horror and heroism of this momentous affair. Something somber and macabre that speaks of four dead and one dying. Perhaps the bodies of the victims in the care of Benjamin

Leigh, a grim mortician, rendered to resemble Thanatos with a long, curved trocar in place of a scythe. Somehow I could mix the red of the British uniforms with the blood red of the wounds, perhaps foreground the holes in the back of James Caldwell to show that unarmed men were gunned down as they fled...no! It is horrible, sensationalist. I am imposing my will upon the scene instead of letting the characters emerge from the canvas and tell their story. Michelangelo described seeing David in a block of marble and cutting away everything which was not the holy man until the statue was revealed. Wipe clean the canvas, Candace Hunter Lee, and remove the white, stroke by stroke, until the soul of this affair speaks its truth.

COLONIST #1: Did you hear the news?

COLONIST #2: Did you see?

COLONIST #3: Were you there?

COLONIST #4: The redcoats fired.

COLONIST #5: Innocent women.

COLONIST #1: Children.

COLONIST #2: Dozens dead.

COLONIST #3: Unprovoked.

COLONIST #4: Skewered with twelve-inch bayonets.

COLONIST #5: John Hancock has called together the Province leaders to issue a declaration of war.

PAINTER: I could perhaps capture the way that news moves through a village, building like fire in fields of straw. It could center on an account of events in the fledgling *Boston Gazette* being read aloud in a village square. I could place a child here, an urchin, peddling pamphlets. A stout man of obvious means might rifle through his purse in search of a copper while a rebellious ruffian fumes in amongst a crowd of his peers while a bespectacled matron reads a description of the deadly deeds to an unwashed hoard of irate illiterates.

MOTHER: *(Reading:)* The Massachusetts Bay Province was made melancholy last evening as news of the murder of four unarmed citizens reached all of the corners of our usually peaceful Colony. British soldiers garrisoned at the Commons of Boston opened fire upon a crowd of protesters who had gathered in response to an altercation between a soldier, identified as Private Hugh White, and an as yet unidentified apprentice wig maker demanding remuneration for commissioned labors. Petitions for arrest have been published against as many as eight of the British contingent, including Captain Thomas Preston. Witnesses offer contradictory accounts of events alternately praising the restraint and condemning the ferocity of the British response. This tragic affair is but the latest in an escalating series of clashes between residents of Boston and the soldiers who many view as an occupation force.

(A SOLDIER paces back and forth until intruding into the scene, then the BRITISH SOLDIERS appear huddled together in a cell.)

SOLDIER: Would you stop pacing and park your parts? You're not walking guard any longer, kid.

SOLDIER: I'm just worried for the Captain.

PVT. KILLROY: You should worry for yourself.

SOLDIER: He's down there alone in court.

PVT. KILLROY: You should be so lucky.

SOLDIER: By that you mean..?

PVT. KILLROY: Are you truly that thick or just afraid to face the wall?

SOLDIER: This prison wears on my patience, so be mindful of how you address me.

PVT. KILLROY: Save it for the magistrate, little as he'll care.

CORPORAL WEEMS: Pipe down the both of you.

SOLDIER: Yes, Corporal.

(Pause.)

CORPORAL WEEMS: The Captain is being tried apart from ourselves so that he can claim we fired in contradiction to his orders.

SOLDIER: Captain Preston would never turnabout like that.

SOLDIER #2: Contradiction?

PVT. MONTGOMERY: Mightn't you, given the chance?

SOLDIER #2: What does contradiction mean in Leicester English?

SOLDIER #3: It means that we hang.

(CAPTAIN PRESTON appears in court as others enact the events of his testimony.)

CAPTAIN PRESTON: If it please the court, I was standing in front of the guns, between my men and their targets. No trained officer who holds life dear would position himself in such a precarious point of vantage unless he expected there would be no gunplay.

(PVT. WHITE strikes a Colonist.)

MAVERICK: You butchering sons of husbandless women!

PVT. WHITE: Move along or you'll get the same.

COLONIST MR. BASS: You keep your distance.

PVT. WHITE: You hold your tongue.

MOTHER CALDWELL: Get a doctor!

ATTUCKS: Try that with me, you prancing dandy.

PVT. WHITE: Stand down, Sirrah.

(Everyone freezes momentarily.)

CAPTAIN PRESTON: An angry mood had been brewing for weeks.

(Characters animate.)

MOTHER CARR: You clapper-round as if thinking you own our streets.

MR. FOSDICK: This is what comes of garrisoning soldiers in Boston proper.

MR. ASHTON: There is not a job to be had from here to Back Bay, what with these stiff-spined snobs picking up extra bob after hours.

MR. FOSDICK: Why else would I be haulin' cord?

ATTUCKS: Give me a firm bit of that. I'm of a mind to clout a prideful peacock.

(Attucks takes a club.)

PVT. WHITE: You will keep your distance or suffer the same as your saucy mate.

(Everyone freezes.)

CAPTAIN PRESTON: *(To audience:)* It was about then that the din reached the barracks and I sallied forth with more soldiers.

(Characters animate.)

(To White:) Remember you are in employ to Her Majesty, lad.

COLONIST #1: That and three leaves will make weak tea.

LIEUTENANT BASSET: Let them rile. You have heard worse —

COLONIST #2: From your hairy lipped wives no doubt.

(Characters freeze.)

CAPTAIN PRESTON: And I dare say that the soldiers showed admirable restraint in the face of vitriolic abuse.

(Enter Captain Goldfinch.)

CAPTAIN GOLDFINCH: What in the name of heaven is going on here?

CAPTAIN PRESTON: The locals are up in arms again.

CAPTAIN GOLDFINCH: On what provocation?

CAPTAIN PRESTON: Anything we do short of turn our masts back toward England is cause enough for this rabble.

CAPTAIN GOLDFINCH: Lieutenant Basset?

LIEUTENANT BASSET: Sir.

CAPTAIN GOLDFINCH: Remind the troops that they are forbidden to fire by province law without written order of a magistrate.

LIEUTENANT BASSET: They have not yet loaded their muskets, but affairs as you can see are risen to a dangerous pitch.

CAPTAIN PRESTON: *(To audience:)* I suspect after two full years of our army's encampment, the hooligans were emboldened by our restraint.

ATTUCKS: Shoot if you dare!

GRAY: Have at us, why do you not?

MOTHER: They only brawl in Dock Street alleys when they have superior numbers.

COLONIST #1: *(Throws snowball:)* Take that for tax, you tosspot.

LOYALIST: Someone rang the Meeting House fire bell and the size of the mob trebled.

(Characters freeze.)

CAPTAIN PRESTON: *(To audience:)* I ordered my men to load muskets and affix bayonets.

PROSECUTOR PAINE: Why would you issue such an order in these circumstances?

LIEUTENANT BASSET: Sir?

CAPTAIN PRESCOTT: Then draw the troops back to the main guardhouse with a great show of preparations; that should at the very least dispel the faint of heart.

(Soldiers load their weapons and affix bayonets.)

MOTHER: Oh my word.

COLONIST: Stand down, fellows!

MOTHER: Come along home, child.

COLONIST: That is enough row for one evening.

CAPTAIN PRESTON: The worst was past, and I was nearly back to the typical level of loathing when a swarthy ruffian snatched a rifle by its mournful end and tried to cudgel one poor private.

(The actions are enacted, guns discharge, screams, panic. The tableau freezes and the Painter appears.)

PAINTER: A strong face. A proud man, but he does not carry through all of the episodes of the story. He was tried and absolved in October in an event apart from his troops. He is not the beating heart of this affair. Painting is painfully easy but selecting the subject, the perspective, the style, that is what makes a master...

(The PROSECUTOR appears and startles the Painter.)

PROSECUTOR PAINE: Most honorable Justices of the court...

COLONIST #1: They were out for blood.

PROSECUTOR PAINE: it is my solemn sworn duty on behalf of the grief-stricken citizens of Boston colony...

COLONIST #2: They wanted revenge for the Ropewalks row.

PROSECUTOR PAINE: to prove both to your satisfaction and the loved ones of our slain kinsmen, that this assemblage of the crown's agents did willfully and with malice in their hearts on the fifth day of May last...

COLONIST #3: I clearly heard the command to fire!

PROSECUTOR PAINE: shoulder their weapons and discharge a deadly fusillade into a defenseless gathering of unarmed men, women and even children.

COLONIST #4: Hanging is too good for the likes of them!

PROSECUTOR PAINE: It is an action so abhorrent...

COLONIST: Hang them!

PROSECUTOR PAINE: so callous...

COLONISTS: Hang them!

PROSECUTOR PAINE: so atypical of the King's representatives...

COLONISTS: Hang them all!

PROSECUTOR PAINE: as to be unequalled in the near centennial history of this colony.

> *(CORPORAL WEEMS appears.)*

CORPORAL WEEMS: I couldn't half recognize myself in the mouths of those monkeys. They magnified every crossed look and gesture until I would have knotted the hangman's noose myself, had the memory of that crown hating mob pressing me back against the unyielding bricks of the Custom House not been as clear in my mind as the crack of the African's skull when he collapsed with two musket balls imbedded in his hale chest.

> *(Rifles fire. Colonists scatter in slow motion leaving one alone narrating events.)*

COLONIST: *(To audience:)* We scattered, I admit it. I ran like the third hog in a slaughter line. You would have done the like; unarmed facing a fusillade. The Commons erupted, and the Brit twits formed close shoulder ranks. I'm retired military myself — served in King Philip's War — and so I recognized the maneuver. We returned for our dead and armed to retaliate, but then Lieutenant Governor Hastings appeared on a balcony above our heads as if called from on high to avert more bloodshed. I cannot say that I was kindly disposed to him prior to that intervention, but he won me to his praise by risking the wrath of that crowd just to save them from themselves.

> *(LT. GOVERNOR HASTINGS appears above.)*

HASTINGS: Colonists, Loyalists, citizens of Boston...

LOYALIST: Thank providence, Governor Hastings has arrived to restore the peace.

HASTINGS: ...our province is shocked and saddened by events of recent hours...

COLONIST #1: The pudding head is as useful as a bent toothed fork.

HASTINGS: ...but we must not allow grief and indignation to inspire more tragic lawlessness.

COLONIST #2: *(To audience:)* Had he not arrived and spoken so forcefully I am certain that the horrendous situation would have been far worse.

HASTINGS: It is too early to knowingly assign blame...

COLONIST #3: Bodies lying twisted in the streets and himself already maneuvering to cover the bright red backs of his master's minions.

HASTINGS: ...but I assure you that this abominable affair will be investigated thoroughly and the guilty punished to the full extent that law allows.

SOLDIER: I don't like the sound of that.

HASTINGS: Please, go back to your homes and trust justice.

COLONIST #4: The windbag thinks he is talking us down, but in fact the muskets of the reinforced British guard arranged in deadly firing formation is a more persuasive argument.

(PATRIOTS appear in separate areas as they testify. Each new line should be delivered by a different member of the chorus.)

PATRIOT CHORUS: I saw...
I saw...
I saw...
I saw...
I heard...

I heard...
I heard...
I heard...
I felt...
I felt...
I felt...
I felt...

(Different chorus members speak each line repeatedly, overlapping each other, until they crescendo in a cacophony of noise. Feel free to organize this chorus and how the lines interact as may suit your cast size and the needs of your production.)

Rifles.
Blood.
Hard voices.
It had been brewing for days.
For weeks.
Since they arrived...
We fear for our daughters.
Savages.
Pompous prigs.
I knew it would come to this.
Cold blooded murder.
Throw them in gaol.
Murder.
Hang them all!
Murder.
Death to King George!

(Patriots should all finish chanting, "Murder.")

PROSECUTOR PAINE: You saw it all, Mrs. Maverick?

MRS. MAVERICK: First to last.

PROSECUTOR PAINE: And your husband?

MRS. MAVERICK: Butchered like a dry milk cow. Samuel Maverick, remember his name you murdering heathens! A better man than the lot of you trussed up together!

(JOHN ADAMS appears seated with a DELEGATION haranguing him. The lines of the following chorus of delegates may be assigned depending on the needs of your production.)

DELEGATION: They will hang them every one, Mr. Adams. The world is watching, Mr. Adams. They cannot all be guilty, Mr. Adams. Are you willing to allow an innocent to die, Mr. Adams? There is fault on both sides, Mr. Adams. King Solomon himself would have been hard pressed, John. You are their only hope, Mr. Adams. Their blood will be on your hands, John, if you wash them of this affair.

(They continue chanting his name as he crosses to the court.)

JOHN ADAMS: They were addressing you harshly, Private White?

PVT. WHITE: Pronouncing against everyone from the Queen through my mother's aunt.

(Crowd animates.)

KID: Take a hearty bite from a worn heeled boot, you British boob.

PVT. WHITE: *(To audience:)* I was not trained a soldier. Like many an unfortunate, I was impressed into service of the crown.

COLONIST #1: Look at him standing there as if his feet had rooted.

KID: I bet I can make him move.

PVT. WHITE: *(To audience:)* What is a man supposed to do when scores of angry rabble set themselves to the task of playing loose with him?

COLONIST #1: Your hat does not hang so high now, boy-o.

COLONIST #2: Give us a bit of your proud British prattle. We like to hear how much better everything is on the other side of the wide water.

COLONIST #3: I suspect he has a salty tongue when a quartet of his mates is standing at his shoulder.

PVT. WHITE: *(To audience:)* Words can cut despite having less weight than a wisp of wind, yet I endured their teasing and kept my tongue until one especially rude fellow set his sights upon one of our Captains.

EDWARD GARRICK: He is a lowborn cur who owes my master for the very wig that he wears crooked on his square head.

PVT. WHITE: *(To audience:)* "Captain Goldfinch," I said, "is an honorable gentleman, and if he received service from your master, then rest assured the fellow will receive his pay." It was my intention to quiet the crowd, but it was as if I had called their fathers Viking marauders.

COLONIST #4: You can grind your Captain Goldfinch, stuff him in a snuffbox and suck him up your nose.

COLONIST #5: Your lot has been taking liberties with our merchants.

COLONIST #1: And our daughters.

COLONIST #5: And flaunting our laws safe behind your bayonets and bluster.

COLONIST #2: But you are not strutting tall this spring evening, are you laddie?

PVT. WHITE: *(To audience:)* Thank providence that Corporal Weems arrived just when matters were poised to turn disastrous.

(Corporal Weems arrives with three soldiers.)

COLONIST #2: Oh, Briton's best come to rescue this milksop.

CORPORAL WEEMS: Report, Private White!

PVT. WHITE: A misunderstanding concerning the payment for a wig for Captain Goldfinch somehow...

CORPORAL WEEMS: All this over a flipping wig?

PVT. KILLROY: It takes but little to incite these dregs...

CORPORAL WEEMS: Did I ask you for tuppence, Killroy?

PVT. KILLROY: No, Corporal.

CORPORAL WEEMS: Go fetch Captain Goldfinch and let's get this madness sorted.

PVT. KILLROY: Yes, Corporal.

(Killroy exits.)

PVT. WHITE: *(To audience:)* Corporal Weems had been everywhere, seen everything and had us in formation, shoulder-to-shoulder, ready to crack skulls if necessary, but just the sight of him was enough to cow that lot.

COLONIST #1: Keep your distance.

ATTUCKS: We haven't a chance against the likes of him.

COLONIST #2: We may as better return to our homes than risk the ire of such a man as that.

PVT. WHITE: *(To audience:)* And we would not be here now nor mourn the dead if the Corporal had been left to his devices, but Killroy returned with Captains Preston and Goldfinch.

(Enter Goldfinch, Preston, soldiers and Killroy.)

CAPTAIN GOLDFINCH: Withdraw at once to the Custom House.

CORPORAL WEEMS: Yes, Captain Goldfinch.

CAPTAIN GOLDFINCH: And advise the men that they may not discharge their weapons without written edict or face prosecution under Province law.

PVT. WHITE: *(To audience:)* You could have done no more hurt had you waved our blood red waistcoats under the nose of a frothing bull.

ATTUCKS: Take heart, friends, the tiger is toothless!

GRAY: I'd wager they haven't even loaded.

PVT. WHITE: *(To audience:)* And that is when the swarthy brute made the error that proved fatal to so many.

(Attucks grabs at a rifle.)

ATTUCKS: You're as harmless as my sister's kitten, aren't you now?

(The gun discharges. The events of the massacre are enacted in slow motion according to White's description.)

PVT. WHITE: *(To audience:)* The report of that musket cut through every sound in the Common, and for a moment there was a perfect and complete quiet, and then everything erupted all at once in a single deafening din. Men screaming, children crying, women snatching up their young, soldiers stuffing swatch and powder into muzzles, great hard ice balls all crashing against our chests. Men charged us, others fled then a fusillade set all but the dead and near so racing off into the darkness.

JOHN ADAMS: Private White...Private White...?

(The scene freezes as White awakens.)

PVT. WHITE: Is that all?

(Private White disappears.)

JOHN ADAMS: If it please the court, the defense calls Christopher Monk.

(MONK appears, walking on crutches.)

CHRISTOPHER MONK: God, by whose graces I have survived to tell this tale, can bear witness to the truth of what I here say. The affair at the Custom House had its start a full week before when a brace of boastful bobbin-heads came cross an unbending group of our best in a local pub. Words became oaths, became pushes, then pushes punches, and the British twits took a proper pounding.

GRAY: That will teach you to keep your turned up noses out of our pubs.

COLONISTS: Huzzah!

BROADERS: I did not know a lobster could scurry so fast.

INNKEEPER: And we are expected to pay tax and abeyance for the likes of that to protect the likes of ourselves.

COLONIST #1: They make laws across an ocean with no advocate for our interest at court.

COLONIST #2: Sod George, Parliament and every other anybody who plots to steal my precious tuppence.

LOYALIST BAILEY: In fairness, we must concede that we relied upon British troops in our wars with the French and the Indians.

ATTUCKS: You will not long sit in that chair sipping mead if you take sides with the pimples that pollute the face of our fair city.

LOYALIST BAILEY: It is not taking sides to admit the truth of our debt to the country that birthed us.

GRAY: I set forth from Ireland, thank you much, and have nothing but a thumb for every Brit on either side of the wide water.

COLONIST #3: And I have nothing kind to say for the royal navy that threats to conscript me into service every time their shadow falls upon my mast.

LOYALIST BAILEY: Do you think we would long enjoy this great city if we were left to stand alone with the French to the north of us and savages to the west?

ATTUCKS: No Frog ever bent me to a task without paying proper wage and those you call savages have fought as I imagine any man might should a stranger occupy his land.

CHRISTOPHER MONK: And they bandied back and forth after that fashion well into night. Then less than a week more on Monday March five, a quarrelsome gang of button-breasted blackguards came cudgeling heads in the alleys near Dock Street.

(British Soldiers threaten citizens.)

COLONIST #1: Do you mean to kill someone this evening?

SOLDIER: We mean to crack any crown that casts its ferret-faced shadow across our path.

SOLDIER: You would be wise to crawl back into your hutch.

COLONIST #1: You have no right to order us off of our streets.

(Soldier strikes him.)

SOLDIER: Here is your right and your left. Now go cry to someone who cares.

JOHN ADAMS: Did you witness this barbarity with your own eye?

CHRISTOPHER MONK: Not just as it happened but shortly after.

JOHN ADAMS: And so the tale could have been altered.

CHRISTOPHER MONK: Anything is possible, Mr. Adams —

JOHN ADAMS: Precisely, therefore I will ask you to confine your comments exclusively to what you personally witnessed.

CHRISTOPHER MONK: It will not leave much to report.

JOHN ADAMS: That is for the court to decide. Close your eyes.

CHRISTOPHER MONK: Beg pardon?

JOHN ADAMS: Close your eyes, please, Mr. Monk...Now drift back to the moment when you first entered into Custom House Square. Can you hear the sounds?

(Actors begin making the sounds of the commotion.)

CHRISTOPHER MONK: Quite clearly.

JOHN ADAMS: As you turn the corner of King Street, who is haranguing whom?

GARRICK: You may be lords of the earth, but here you are just strutting puffs.

MOTHER: Your welcome is past threadbare worn.

COLONIST #1: And you have no one to blame but yourselves, for from the first you have been racing through our streets raising up a row.

JOHN ADAMS: Mr. Monk?

(The scene freezes.)

I am quite sure that you could go on at great length entering many minute details into the public record, but indulge me to progress ahead to when affairs had heated and a shot was discharged... Did you hear a command to fire?

(Chaos erupts as colonists tussle with the armed soldiers.)

CHRISTOPHER MONK: I very well expect that no one living can with complete certainty identify any single actor in that enormous mob.

ATTUCKS: Shoot! If you have the stones.

CHRISTOPHER MONK: There were so many people yelling all at once, fifty or more townsfolk screaming and pushing, pasty-faced soldiers getting jostled by angry urchins, mothers hurrying their brood out of imminent danger—

JOHN ADAMS: And so it is fair to conclude that the chaos obfuscated the sequence of actions.

CHRISTOPHER MONK: I might conclude that if I knew what it meant.

JOHN ADAMS: We cannot now with certainty identify if the garrisoned soldiers struck out with murderous intent or if they were forced to fire in fear for their lives. Perhaps even if the first shot originated in the threatening crowd or by some unfortunate accident—

CHRISTOPHER MONK: Anything could have happened.

JOHN ADAMS: Thank you, Mr. Monk.

CHRISTOPHER MONK: But I'd like to —

JOHN ADAMS: That will be all...thank you.

(A PATRIOT appears in limbo.)

COLONIST #1: It wouldn't be fair to call the trial a farce. Everything was done in accordance with law and in plain sight. Still, when four unarmed men die on the street stones and another one day after, and all that passes for recompense is a brand upon the thumb of two soldiers, I am wont to call it justice.

(John Adams appears alone.)

JOHN ADAMS: The very last thing that I either wanted or needed was to be engaged to defend British nits who gunned down Boston citizens in plain view of three score witnesses. My modest political aspirations will likely be as dead as Black Crispus by the time this trial is through, and worse, between the lot of them they haven't enough coin to wheel my carriage. If only your conscience could stomach a fool being abused, then you might have made something of yourself in this world, John Adams. Well, spilled milk is not worth mourning.

(Private Killroy appears alone.)

PVT. KILLROY: Dame Justice is indeed blind, but that is not something good. It means that she often cannot see what is right in front of her face. The whole of Boston has called for my head without any knowledge of my character or the crisis that I faced on that fateful Monday. They say I panicked, but unless you were there pressed back against a wall with a burly African leading a chorus of catcalls aimed at everyone east of Plymouth, then you cannot pass fair verdict on my actions.

JUDGE: What say you, jury?

JURY: In the case of the Province of Boston versus Private Hugh Montgomery in the death of Crispus Attucks, we find the defendant guilty of murder.

JUDGE: What say you, jury?

JURY: In the case of the Massachusetts Bay Province versus Private Hugh White in the death of Crispus Attucks, we find the defendant not guilty.

JUDGE: What say you, jury.

JURY: In the case of the Massachusetts Bay Province versus Hammond Green in the death of Crispus Attucks, we find the defendant not guilty.

JUDGE: What say you, jury.

JURY: In the case of the Massachusetts Bay Province versus John Carroll in the death of James Caldwell, we find the defendant not guilty.

JUDGE: What say you, jury.

JURY: In the case of the Massachusetts Bay Province versus Lieutenant James Basset in the death of Patrick Carr, we find the defendant not guilty.

JURY: In the case of the Massachusetts Bay Province versus Corporal William Weems, we find the defendant not guilty of murder.

JUDGE: What say you, jury.

JURY: In the case of the Massachusetts Bay Province versus Private Matthew Killroy in the death of Crispus Attucks, we find the defendant guilty of murder.

CROWD: Huzzah!!! Justice! Serves you right! Now you'll get your proper comeuppance! God be praised!

JUDGE: Order! Order! Or I will have this chamber cleared.

JUDGE #2: You will not repeat the unruly behavior that precipitated this trial in the first place.

(The Judge gavels them into silence.)

JUDGE #3: Before sentencing, Privates Montgomery and Killroy, is there anything that you would like to say to the court?

PVT. MONTGOMERY: May it please your honors, as a military man I have been taught to respect authority. So I accept your judgment, ignoring any sentiment that I may harbor concerning my actions. The evidence has been presented, measured, and the decree does not favor my cause. There is nothing for me to do but submit.

JUDGE #3: Private Killroy?

PVT. KILLROY: Mercy upon me, O God, according to thy loving kindness: according unto the multitude of thy tender mercies, blot out my transgressions.

(TOWNSPEOPLE appear in a separate area.)

TOWNSMAN #1: He just started reading from the Bible.

TOWNSMAN #2: Reciting more likely.

PVT. KILLROY: Wash me thoroughly from mine iniquity, and cleanse me from my sin.

TOWNSMAN #3: I suppose he turned to God facing the noose.

PVT. KILLROY: For I acknowledge my transgressions: and my sin is ever before me.

TOWNSMAN #2: That's it by half and half only.

JUDGE: *(In courtroom:)* As a full citizen of England here in service of our country, the court concedes that Private Killroy is indeed within his rights to invoke Benefit of Clergy, and the charge is hereby reduced to manslaughter.

TOWNSMAN #1: Benefit of Clergy?

TOWNSMAN #3: What in the name of justice is that?

(Private White appears with a Bible.)

PVT. MONTGOMERY: Mercy upon me, O God, according to thy loving kindness: according unto the multitude of thy tender mercies blot out my transgressions.

TOWNSMAN #1: Is he saying that he's a parson?

TOWNSMAN #3: And if he is, what of it?

SERVING WOMAN: Then he will get away with murder.

TOWNSMAN #1: The devil you say!

TOWNSMAN #2: She speaks truth.

SERVING WOMAN: I stand here living proof of this curious law.

TOWNSMAN #1: You have taken a life?

SERVING WOMAN: My Grand Da's goat caused a cross of words with a disagreeable neighbor that was settled with a dirk. I am here stirring pots today because the old fox recited the same passage in a British court.

TOWNSMAN #3: Are we to believe that a man of the cloth cannot murder?

INNKEEPER: When Henry fought against the church, the clergy claimed to be apart from civil law.

SERVING WOMAN: Then clever fellows like my Grand Da took to claiming benefit of clergy when they got pinched.

TOWNSMAN #3: So why are the British gaols so full that they're sending their flotsam here to torment our shores?

INNKEEPER: Because you can only claim the privilege once.

TOWNSMAN #3: So any blaggard who can read from the good book goes bird free?

(The Judge appears in a separate area.)

JUDGE: In accordance with precedent of law the charges are hereby reduced to manslaughter and punishable by the branding of the letter "M" on the thumb of each convicted defendant.

(Shadow shows Private Killroy being branded with an M. The scream of pain turns into the screech of a bagpipe. A procession enters carrying coffins.)

REVEREND: Friends, bereaved relatives, citizens of Boston Province, we are called together in these sad times to lay to rest five unfortunate men—

COLONIST #1: A single grave?

REVEREND: men struck down and sent to glory long before their promised four score and ten—

COLONIST #2: Why are they being buried together?

REVEREND: The times threaten to count these few but the first among many who may paint these streets with blood and teardrop in defense of the rights of the British abroad—

COLONIST #3: America for the Americans!

SHERIFF: Let's not forget the solemn purpose that collects us together on this morning and instead save our politics for another day.

COLONIST #3: Of course you would say as much, Sheriff, seeing as you have been broken like a housedog by your British masters.

SHERIFF: Place that thought in a rear room of your mind until after this service, and I will be sure to revisit it with you behind the ropewalks.

REVEREND: If your stomach is not filled past full with hate, if your heart is not shattered by the loss of innocent life, at least have compassion for the mothers, wives, sons and daughters who are assembled here to pay their last respects to the departed. *(Pause.)* And so we lay these souls to rest and pray that each will find the peace that is denied to all in this sinful world of woe.

ALL: Amen.

(Characters disperse leaving Captain Preston standing in front of the Customs House.)

CAPTAIN PRESTON: I feared that the true intentions of this unruly mob was the Custom House, wherein rested quite a tidy sum of the King's gold, and I vowed before heaven that I would kill every man Jack before one single coin would be removed by this unwashed lot.

(Preston freezes in a pose from Revere's etching.)

PVT. MONTGOMERY: Disobey an order and they bring you up on charges. Obey a command and they burn an "M" upon your thumb.

(Captain Garrick appears.)

GARRICK: To think that this whole sordid tragedy began over a dispute about a flipping wig. Had I known it would come to this unhappy state of affairs then I would have paid the petit tyrant twice and been done with it.

(Garrick takes his pose in the etching. A SEAMAN appears in the Rope Walk.)

SEAMAN: Here's to Crispus Attucks, as true a mate as any whaler could ask for. He come from nothing and never made much, but his word was as stout as well wound hemp and there was no better soul could stand to my left in a row, bless his swarthy hide.

(Seaman takes his pose. The Young Kid appears.)

KID: I thought the whole of it marvelous fun at the first. The soldiers had been horribly rude for ever so long. They liked to race their horses right outside our church on Sunday morning and strike up a row on every imagined provocation. A trio of them had pummeled my Da when he called them ill bred for making comment on my mother's bodice. The chance to feed them a bit of hard packed snow and sharp words went down well on Monday evening until the shooting started.

(Young Kid takes pose.)

MOTHER: When the whooping is done, long after some new flag flies above the house of state, I and other mothers will sit alone and mourn our sacrificed sons.

(The Painter appears and begins moving the bodies as if each were composed of color, arranging them into a portrait of the massacre.)

PAINTER: This might just be another in a litany of indignities. If, however, oil and canvas can somehow enlarge the meaning of events, then I will use every color on my palate to capture the spirit of this tragedy. I must affix the pigments so that other men in distant locales can rise above the tyranny of detail and appreciate the grand collision of disaffected colonists and isolated, over-proud, soldiers caught on the wrong side of a movement toward independence. A movement as inexorable as the thaw that follows in the wake of every winter.

(The completed tableau is revealed and then lights fade to black. The end.)

The Author Speaks

What inspired you to write this play?
One of the exercises that I often do during school workshops is to create a three-scene play that illustrates some idea elicited from the class. Students shared that they had just started the Revolutionary War section of the semester and the event that they selected to dramatize was the Boston Massacre. I had visited Boston Commons during a tour of the city, and I was moved by the dramatic possibilities of a story that shaped a nation.

Was the structure of the play influenced by any other work?
I know that I wanted the freedom to move through the events of this sprawling story in non-linear fashion. Again I turned to my classroom exercises. This time I used "Painter," which is a game wherein one youth creates a portrait of a historical event by physically manipulating the bodies of other students (i.e. the colors).

Have you dealt with the same theme in other works that you have written?
The Boston Massacre is unique among my body of plays but it does draw on elements that I have used in various projects. Thematically it revisits my modern verse play, **Mountain.** In that earlier opus work, I used the battle of King's Mountain to demonstrate the folly of war. Both sides are culpable, and everyone manipulates the facts in an attempt to position themselves in the role of either hero or victim. The character of Crispus Attucks appeared in a short play called **Crispus Attucks at the Liberty Bell.** I learned during research for that work that he may not have been the noble patriot that modern American history has suggested. Conversely, it has also been argued that the early unfavorable depictions of this African

American martyr were altered because of racial bias. The realities of his personality and deeds are now forever obscured. This inspired me to use the Roshomon effect in *The Boston Massacre*. The Captain recalls one series of events when on trial. while the soldiers who are imprisoned awaiting their day in court remember their actions differently.

What writers have had the most profound effect on your style?
In my twenties while living in Chicago for the two-year run of *A Nite In The Life Of Bessie Smith* (aka *Little Miss Dreamer*), I used to escape the ravenous cold by passing days in the library. There I would read the entire canon of a single author as well as a biography and any letters or personal writing that I could find. I did this with Lorraine Hansberry, Tennessee Williams, Eugene O'Neill, Georg Büchner and others. Every play that I write is therefore influenced by those writers. The strongest single influence on *The Boston Massacre* however is YouthPLAYS co-founder Jon Dorf. Very little of my writing prior to joining this company had been created for young actors. My commission writing for major youth theatres was still primarily adult casts collaborating with young professional actors. Conversations with Jon introduced me to the unique genre of plays for young actors. I have relied on him heavily to help indoctrinate me into the unique rules of this specialized theatrical form.

What do you hope to achieve with this work?
The Boston Massacre is educational theatre. First and foremost the experience of working on it is intended to inspire in depth research into this important moment in world history. This is part of the current middle school academic curriculum brought to life. I will feel successful if audiences are entertained and inspired to explore the sanguine events of

March 5, 1770.

What inspired you to become a playwright?
As a young man, life taught me that "the right word in the right ear at the right time can change the world." I became a playwright in order to speak the words, "love," "truth," "tolerance," and "courage."

Are any characters modeled after real life or historical figures?
I researched this play much less exhaustively than most of my previous historical works. Usually I consult primarily original sources and seek out the authors of key books and articles that I uncover. The fact that this is an expressionistic play set in the mind of the painter frees me to present the facts as her mind remembers them. She is not a historian and mostly concerned with finding an interesting visual image for her project. I tried to therefore approach research in the same ways that she would. I relied heavily on internet sites and allowed the contradictions between them to lead me to books as well as correspondences with friends who were history teachers.

Do any film versions of this play exist?
No films yet exist of *The Boston Massacre* because the play is awaiting its premiere. It is my intention to grant permission for this inaugural production to film both rehearsals and performances and then have the material edited into a film

About the Author

Ed Shockley, MFA is author of more than 70 plays. His works have set five box office records and been honored with numerous awards, including the Stephen Sondheim Award for Outstanding Contributions to American Musical Theatre, a

Pew Fellowship in the Arts and PA State Arts Council
Playwrights Fellowship. He has received commissions for
youth theatre plays from Seattle Children's Theatre, Children's
Theatre of Charlotte, Dallas Children's Theatre, Black
Spectrum Theatre and the Harlem Renaissance Theatre. His
historical short film, *Stone Mansion*, aired on Showtime
television. Website: http://edshockley.com.

About YouthPLAYS

YouthPLAYS (www.youthplays.com) is a publisher of award-winning professional dramatists and talented new discoveries, each with an original theatrical voice, and all dedicated to expanding the vocabulary of theatre for young actors and audiences. On our website you'll find one-act and full-length plays and musicals for teen and pre-teen (and even college) actors, as well as duets and monologues for competition. Many of our authors' works have been widely produced at high schools and middle schools, youth theatres and other TYA companies, both amateur and professional, as well as at elementary schools, camps, churches and other institutions serving young audiences and/or actors worldwide. Most are intended for performance by young people, while some are intended for adult actors performing for young audiences.

YouthPLAYS was co-founded by professional playwrights Jonathan Dorf and Ed Shockley. It began merely as an additional outlet to market their own works, which included a substantial body of award-winning published and unpublished plays and musicals. Those interested in their published plays were directed to the respective publishers' websites, and unpublished plays were made available in electronic form. But when they saw the desperate need for material for young actors and audiences—coupled with their experience that numerous quality plays for young people weren't finding a home—they made the decision to represent the work of other playwrights as well. Dozens and dozens of authors are now members of the YouthPLAYS family, with scripts available both electronically and in traditional acting editions. We continue to grow as we look for exciting and challenging plays and musicals for young actors and audiences.

About ProduceaPlay.com

Let's put up a play! Great idea! But producing a play takes time, energy and knowledge. While finding the necessary time and energy is up to you, ProduceaPlay.com is a website designed to assist you with that third element: knowledge.

Created by YouthPLAYS' co-founders, Jonathan Dorf and Ed Shockley, ProduceaPlay.com serves as a resource for producers at all levels as it addresses the many facets of production. As Dorf and Shockley speak from their years of experience (as playwrights, producers, directors and more), they are joined by a group of award-winning theatre professionals and experienced teachers from the world of academic theatre, all making their expertise available for free in the hope of helping this and future generations of producers, whether it's at the school or university level, or in community or professional theatres.

The site is organized into a series of major topics, each of which has its own page that delves into the subject in detail, offering suggestions and links for further information. For example, Publicity covers everything from Publicizing Auditions to How to Use Social Media to Posters to whether it's worth hiring a publicist. Casting details Where to Find the Actors, How to Evaluate a Resume, Callbacks and even Dealing with Problem Actors. You'll find guidance on your Production Timeline, The Theater Space, Picking a Play, Budget, Contracts, Rehearsing the Play, The Program, House Management, Backstage, and many other important subjects.

The site is constantly under construction, so visit often for the latest insights on play producing, and let it help make your play production dreams a reality.

More from YouthPLAYS

A Stranger on the Bus by Ed Shockley
Drama. About 120 minutes. Flexible cast of 12-50.

The audience experiences the landmark Swann v. Board of Education case that completed the integration of American schools through the dream of a young African-American girl injured in a public school riot. With Jim Crow appearing in the guise of a giant trickster bird to battle the forces of progress, this award-winning epic begins at World War II and journeys to the moment when two innocent children can sit side by side en route to a new era in our nation's history.

The Legend of Sleepy Hollow by Jonathan Josephson
Adaptation. 25-30 minutes. 4+ males, 1+ females, 4+ either (5-15 performers possible).

A theatrical adaptation of Washington Irving's timeless tale of Ichabod Crane, the fair damsel Katrina Van Tassel, and the most feared spectre of the realm, the Headless Horseman of Sleepy Hollow. An ideal Halloween story that's a pleasure all year long for lovers of literature and theatre!

The Old New Kid by Adam J. Goldberg
Comedy. 30-40 minutes. 2-9+ males, 3-10+ females (8-30+ performers possible).

It's the half-day of school before Thanksgiving break, and current "new kid" Alan Socrates Bama just wants to get through the day. But when a new-new kid arrives, things change. Alan has three hours to find the meaning of Thanksgiving, survive elementary school politics, battle for his identity, and spell the word "cornucopia" in this *Peanuts*-flavored comedy for kids of all ages.

Midsummer.com by Flip Kobler and Cindy Marcus
Comedy. 70-80 minutes. 5-11+ males, 10-16+ females (15-35+ performers possible).

Titania and Oberon just can't make it work. In a fit of mutually jealous rage they inadvertently zap themselves and all the fairies into our very real world—right into the middle of a teen summer theatre camp that's mounting ***A Midsummer Night's Dream***. Now Puck and the fairies must find a way to reignite the love between their king and queen, or the whole group will be stuck here forever. But love is not as simple as it first appears. And with real life mirroring the Bard's greatest comedy, it'll take more than a little magic to get Cupid to hit the right targets.

Telling William Tell by Evan Guilford-Blake
Dramedy. 80-85 minutes. 7-11 males, 4-10 females (11-21 performers possible).

The children grab the spotlight in this retelling of the story of the mythical Swiss hero—famed for shooting an apple off his son's head—framed by a fictionalized story of Rossini writing his famed opera. Music by the great composer enriches this thrilling tale of Switzerland's fight for freedom and the birth of a new work of musical art.

The Snow Globe by Sara Crawford
Fantasy for Young Audiences. 90-100 minutes. 4-5 females, 2-3 males (7 performers total).

Young Tabatha finds a snow globe in the woods, but she soon discovers that this isn't just any snow globe: a witch has created her own world inside and "populated" it with talking dolls, a cunning cat, an honorable crow—and now she's captured a boy from Tabatha's neighborhood. If Tabatha is going to keep Ethan from being turned into a doll forever, it'll take more than just overcoming the obstacles inside the globe: they'll need to face the ones outside as well.

46806287R00025

Made in the USA
Middletown, DE
09 August 2017